C is for Ciao

An Italy Alphabet

Written by Elissa D. Grodin and Governor Mario M. Cuomo

Illustrated by Marco Ventura

Italy

A Message by Governor Mario M. Cuomo

The United States of America has been blessed with valuable natural resources. But our greatest blessing has been the generations of immigrants who have come to our land from all over the world, eager to make their contribution to our growing country in return for the chance to earn a good life. They have made us the most spectacularly diverse nation in the world.

Some Americans believed that we should think of these newcomers to our land as being dropped into a "melting pot" that could boil away their distinguishing cultures, homogenizing them into a new multiethnic America. I have always believed that the better analogy for America would be the mosaic, like those in many church windows, each a different size, shape, and color, harmoniously arranged to form beautiful patterns. It would be tragic if our country were to sacrifice the immigrants' gifts in favor of some kind of bland uniformity. I see America as a magnificent new nation of people who have come here bringing with them reflections of their own distinct cultures, joining with the people and traditions already here. Our beauty is in the harmonizing—not the homogenizing—of our people.

Imagine how great a loss it would be if we erased from our culture the reflections of architecture and skill that built the aqueducts, the paintings and brilliance of da Vinci and Michelangelo, the operas, the science, the literature, the fashion, the cuisine, and the thousands of years of history. Those are all gifts that have been brought to us and preserved for us largely by Italians, and that have now become important parts of our open-armed American culture that absorbs, adopts, and shares freely the offerings of all people who have come here seeking to be part of the dazzling "American Mosaic."

The word "aqueduct" comes from the ancient Roman language of Latin, and means "conveyor of water." Aqueducts were used in ancient Rome (which, according to legend, was founded in 753 BC), and continue to be built today. The purpose of these channels or trenches is to carry large amounts of fresh water to populated areas where water is needed. Roman aqueducts were not only useful but also architecturally beautiful. Their remains provide evidence of the ancients' brilliance as engineers and builders. Sections of some original brick and stone aqueducts built thousands of years ago are still standing. By way of comparison, how old is the oldest building or bridge where you live?

The ancient Roman Empire lasted until around AD 400, and was one of the largest empires ever known to the world. It refers not just to the city of that name, but to the entire boot-shaped peninsula that is modern-day Italy. As you will see, the ancient Roman civilization had a lasting impact on the world. Roman law paved the way for the legal systems of many countries today. Latin, the language of ancient Rome, is the basis for all Romance languages. The ingenuity of Roman engineering provided building models for thousands of years to come.

Aa

A is for the Aqueducts
that had to be quite strong,
built to last with bricks and stone
to carry fresh water along.

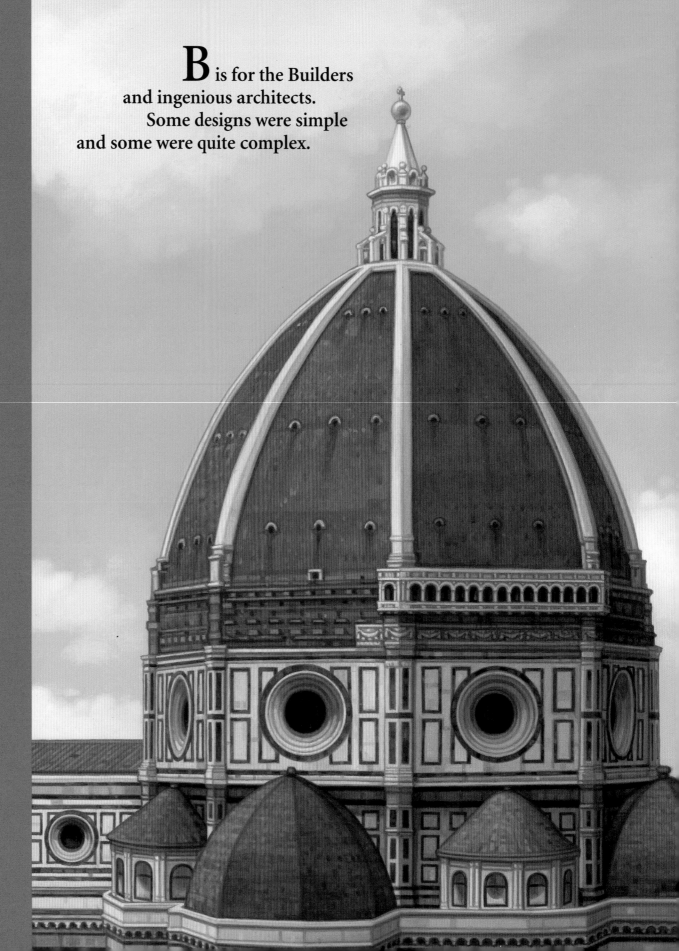

B b

B is for the Builders
and ingenious architects.
Some designs were simple
and some were quite complex.

When people visit Italy they are astonished by its unrivaled beauty. The buildings of Italy cover a span of almost three thousand years. Just as with painting, music, fashion, or even language, architecture evolves over time and expresses itself through different styles. Classical, Romanesque (Abbey of Pomposa), Gothic (the Doge's Palace in Venice), and Baroque (Piazza of St. Peter's in Rome), describe various periods in the history of Italian architecture.

Renaissance architecture was especially pleasing and successful (Renaissance is a French word meaning "rebirth," but we will talk more about this later.) Filippo Brunelleschi (1377-1446), along with other Renaissance architects, studied ancient Roman design and imitated its classical style and construction. The Pantheon (done in the Classical style) is the oldest building in Rome and was his favorite ancient structure. Brunelleschi designed the famous dome for the cathedral—or *duomo*—in Florence. His designs had an enormous influence on Italian architecture.

St. Peter's Basilica in Rome is considered to be the jewel in the crown of Renaissance architecture. The *basilica* (church) was originally designed by Donato Bramante (1444-1514), another highly influential architect.

Doge's Palace, Venice

Mole Antonelliana, Turin

Sicilian Temple, Selinunte

Tower of Pisa, Pisa

Chartreuse of Pavia, Pavia

St. Peter's Basilica, Rome

Abbey of Pomposa, Pomposa

Palladian Villa Porto, Malo

Esposizione Universale Roma, Rome

Andrea Palladio's (1508–1580) style was imitated throughout Europe for hundreds of years. Known for his villas and palaces, the adjective "palladian" is still used by designers and architects today.

Construction began on the famous Leaning Tower of Pisa—*La Torre Pendente di Pisa*—in 1173. Built of white marble in the Romanesque style, its architect is unknown. This bell tower, or *campanile*, is part of the Cathedral of Pisa, a group of three buildings that also includes the cathedral and the baptistry. The tower is leaning because its foundation was built on sandy, unstable soil. Over recent years, engineers were able to lessen the tower's lean by 14 inches and make it safe for the public to visit.

Italian words are beautiful.
Why not learn some now?
A useful little word to know
that starts with C is *Ciao*!

Italian is part of the group of languages known as Romance languages. Italian developed from the ancient language of Latin, the official language of the Roman Empire. People who spoke Latin were described as "speaking in the Roman way," and that is how the term "Romance language" came to be. The other languages in this group are French, Spanish, Portuguese, and Romanian.

As Italian gradually evolved from Latin, many regional dialects developed throughout Italy. Eventually the Tuscan dialect became the accepted Italian language. Dante Alighieri (1265–1321), a philosopher and writer from Florence, helped standardize the spoken language by being one of the first to use it—instead of the traditional Latin—in his writing. His masterpiece, *The Divine Comedy*, was an immediate best-seller.

Words, like people, all come from somewhere. More than half the words in the English dictionary come from Latin words. For example, the word "verdict" comes from the Latin words *vere*—meaning "truly"—and *dictum*—meaning "spoken."

The identity of the woman who modeled for Leonardo da Vinci's painting, the *Mona Lisa*, was debated for hundreds of years until the riddle was finally solved. Historians agree that the sitter was most probably Lisa Gherardini. In addition to its great beauty, what makes this portrait perhaps the most famous painting in the world is the mysterious nature of the sitter's expression, whose meaning captivates and provokes our imaginations.

Leonardo (1452–1519) was born in Vinci, near Florence. He was a gifted child and a rare genius. When he was 14 he became apprenticed to the painter and sculptor Andrea del Verrocchio. Leonardo became accomplished in painting, drawing, sculpting, anatomy, botany, architecture, aeronautics, optics, and music, and pushed boundaries of knowledge further than was imaginable. His drawings and designs anticipated many future inventions, such as helicopters, airplanes, bicycles, and submarines. His extendable ladder is still used by firefighters today.

Artists in the centuries to follow Leonardo are still strongly influenced and inspired by him. The twentieth-century artist Andy Warhol produced a remarkable series of paintings and silk screens based on the *Last Supper* and the *Mona Lisa*.

D is for Da Vinci
who gained the admiration
of people 'round the world
and a genius reputation.

E e

E is for Emperor Augustus—
The first in a great, long line
of rulers of the Empire,
before its unlucky decline.

Rome was ruled by emperors for 400 years, beginning in the year 27 BC, which marked the beginning of the era known as the Roman Empire. The first emperor was Augustus Caesar (63 BC–AD 14).

Emperor Augustus worked hard to bring peace and prosperity after years of civil war. As well as building new aqueducts and bridges, he was a patron of literature and the arts. Augustus created jobs for poor people and helped to improve their lives. Augustus established the Praetorian Guard, which performed the same duty as the president's Secret Service does today.

Today the government in Italy is a Parliamentary democracy. Two houses of Parliament—the Chamber of Deputies and the Senate—have equal power in passing laws. A president is elected to a seven-year term, and he or she appoints the Prime Minister, who must be approved by Parliament. The Prime Minister, who has no fixed term of office and can be voted out by Parliament, is the one who sets national policy.

Ff

When people got fed up with the gloominess of the Middle Ages, a new period emerged—an era of joy of learning and discovery. This was the Renaissance (1300s–1600), and it all began in the city of Florence.

A painter in Florence is credited with starting the Renaissance. Giotto (1266–1337) was the first artist to paint nature and people in a realistic and natural way, instead of in the traditional idealized way. Giotto (pronounced "jotto") understood the value and importance of portraying the world as it really appears. In his frescoes (paintings on damp plaster) Giotto tried to show people's real emotions. Other painters, inspired and excited by this new way, followed his example and began painting in a more naturalistic style.

Florence is the capital of the region of Tuscany. This uniquely beautiful city with a skyline dominated by Brunelleschi's *duomo* lies on both banks of the Arno River, and at the foot of the Apennine Mountains. The splendid Ponte Vecchio is the only bridge in Florence to survive the devastation and bombing of World War II. Spanning the Arno River and lined with shops, it was designed by Taddeo Gaddi, a student of Giotto, and built in 1345.

F is for the city of Florence
whose importance is no mystery.
As the birthplace of the Renaissance,
it stands alone in history.

The enormous Pitti Palace was designed by Brunelleschi. The Pitti banking family built it to compete with the wealthy Medici family. Construction began in 1457, but when building costs eventually bankrupted the Pitti family, the Medici bought it. Today it is a museum filled with treasures from the Medici collection.

Before Italy was unified into one country in 1861, the Republic of Italy was made up of city-states, each with its own government and cultural traditions. Florence was ruled by the wealthy and powerful Medici family, who made their fortune in banking. Their rule lasted from the early 1400s to 1737, except for two short periods of time. Guided by cultural interests, the Medici were generous patrons of the arts, and helped artists like Michelangelo and Raphael make Florence an important center of art.

Gg

Until the Polish astronomer Nicolaus Copernicus (1473–1543) discovered that the sun is the center of our solar system, around which the planets orbit, people since the second century had thought the sun revolved around the earth. The earth was considered to be the center of our solar system.

Galileo Galilei (1564–1642) was born in Pisa and was an astronomer, mathematician, and physicist. In developing the telescope, Galileo was able to prove that Copernicus's theory was correct. This caused a problem with church leaders of the day, who—disrespectful of scientific facts—were offended by the idea that the earth was not the center of the solar system. They placed Galileo under house arrest for the rest of his life.

Galileo's discoveries were not limited to astronomy. He invented a geometric compass which was used as the first pocket calculator. He hired an instrument maker to mass-produce this invention. He also invented a pendulum-controlled clock, which doctors could use to measure a patient's pulse.

G is for Galileo,
　punished when he proved
that the sun was sitting still
　　and the earth's the one that moved.

H is for Italy's Heritage,
  from artwork to invention.
A treasure trove of gifts to us,
    too many to even mention.

Italy's cultural influence on art and design, language and literature, politics, medicine, and science is immeasurable. It is practically impossible to contemplate the worlds of music, or painting, or architecture without Italy's contributions.

Inventors and innovators abound. In thirteenth-century Venice the first pair of eyeglasses was recorded. Harpsichord maker Bartolomeo Cristofori (1655–1731) built the first piano around 1709. Incredibly, two of his pianos still exist. One is in the Metropolitan Museum of Art in New York City. Alessandro Volta (1745–1827) invented the electric cell battery in 1800. The word "volt" (a unit of measure for electricity) comes from his name. Guglielmo Marconi (1874–1937) received the Nobel Prize for Physics in 1909 for his work in radio waves. Enrico Fermi (1901–1954) built the first nuclear reactor and also received the Nobel Prize for Physics.

Italy's prominence in the world of design is legendary, too. Just behold the beauty and grace of a Vespa, the classic motorized scooter.

h
H

Ii

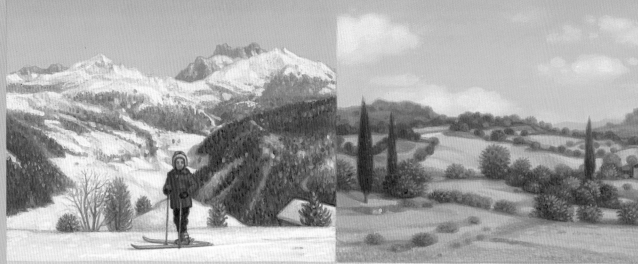

Alps

Apennine Mountains

Italy—*Italia*, from the ancient Romans—is a peninsula in southern Europe that extends into the Mediterranean Sea. It borders France, Switzerland, Austria, and Slovenia. The Apennine Mountains run like a backbone down almost the whole length of Italy. The Po Valley is the richest agricultural region in Italy. It is also the most densely populated area. The Po River, Italy's longest river, drains into the Adriatic Sea.

Including the islands of Sicily and Sardinia, Italy is made up of eight land regions: the **Alpine Slope**, the **Po Valley**, the **Adriatic Plain**, the **Apennines**, **Apulia** and the **Southeastern Plains**, and the **Western Uplands** and **Plains**.

"Sunny Italy" actually contains a wide variety of weather that falls within three general areas. In the northern region of the Alps the summers are warm and rainy and the winters are cold, whereas dry summers and freezing, damp winters characterize the Po Valley area. As for the rest of Italy, long, hot summers and mild winters provide a lovely climate.

The official name of Italy is *Repubblica Italiana*. The national anthem is "Inno di Mameli" ("Mameli's Hymn"). The currency is the euro, which replaced the Italian lira in 2002.

Tyrrhenian Coast

Lake Como

Po River

Stromboli Volcano

I is for *Italia*–
From mountaintops to beaches,
from olive groves to island coves,
and farmlands ripe with peaches.

Italy is made up of 20 political regions, each with its own local government. The various regions provide an amazing diversity of dialects, cuisine, architecture, and landscape. For example, French and German are spoken as first languages in parts of northwestern Italy. Studies of the dialects in the far south have revealed evidence of traces of the ancient Greek language. Sometimes the rough and isolating landscape of an area has helped preserve old-fashioned ways in small, hard-to-reach communities.

The official Italian *tri-colore* flag of green, white, and red was first used in 1796. Designed by Napoleon Bonaparte, who helped remove Austrian rule from northern Italy, the flag is based on the French flag.

Curiously, there are two independent countries within Italy; tiny San Marino in the north, and Vatican City in Rome.

Good writing illuminates life so that we can better understand the world around us, as well as better understand ourselves. Cicero's work (106–43 BC; *De Republica)* helped shape philosophical thinking through the ages. The poetry of Virgil (70–19 BC; *Aeneid)* and Horace (65–8 BC; *Odes*) is still studied and admired today. Juvenal's satirical poems (*Satires*) shed light on problems of his day by making fun of certain aspects of Roman society. He lived around AD 60–AD 130.

Niccolo Machiavelli (1469–1527; *The Prince*) is considered to be the father of modern political science, the study of governments. Filippo Mazzei (1730–1816) was a physician, scholar, horticulturalist, and political writer. He traveled to America and became friends with Thomas Jefferson. Jefferson translated Mazzei's words, "All men are by nature equally free and independent," and used them in the Declaration of Independence as "All men are created equal." Carlo Collodi (1826–1890) wrote the children's classic, *The Adventures of Pinocchio.* Luigi Pirandello (1867–1936) won the Nobel Prize for his philosophical plays, *Six Characters in Search of an Author.* Primo Levi (1919–1987) wrote about his experiences as a prisoner in a Nazi concentration camp during World War II (*If This Is a Man*).

J j

J is for writers like Juvenal
who bring a point of view
to illuminate our lives and world
and show us something new.

K k

K is for the Kitchen
where foods that we create
bring us all together
to enjoy and appreciate.

Eating is a fine example of the Italian gift for making art out of everyday life. Mealtime creates family togetherness, emphasizes the importance of tradition and history, and brings generations together in happy activity.

The cornerstone of Italian cooking is the use of good quality, fresh, local ingredients. The great American chef, Mario Batali, puts it this way: "Perfectly pristine (fresh) ingredients, combined sensibly and cooked properly, are what make Italian food taste so good, both in Italy and in the U.S."

Most dishes are simple, and allow the flavors of the fresh ingredients to shine through, without any single flavor overpowering the others. Think of some of the delightful foods we enjoy, courtesy of Italy—spaghetti with tomato sauce, macaroni, pasta, minestrone, pizza, lasagna—just to name a few.

Pasta dishes are common as a first course, followed by meat, fish, or poultry, and one or two vegetables. Here are translations of a few pastas:

Tortellini: *little cakes*
Linguine: *little tongues*
Ravioli: *little turnips*
Fettuccine: *little ribbons*
Farfalle: *butterflies*
Spaghetti: *little strings*
Orecchiette: *little ears*
Vermicelli: *little worms*
Rotelle: *little wheels*

Cooking in Italy is distinctly—and proudly—regional. One reason is that because Italy did not unify until 1861, each region evolved its own individual identity, of which cuisine played a big part. Just about every town boasts a signature dish.

Another factor is climate and landscape. Northern Italy has pastureland and plains where cows are raised. Because of this, beef, veal, and butter and cream sauces made from cow's milk are common. In the south where there are no pastures for cows to graze, butter is less common and olive oil is used much more. Tomatoes are a staple in southern cooking because they grow in abundance in the hot, sunny climate.

L 1

On the morning of August 24 in AD 79, the city of Pompeii became frozen in time when nearby Mt. Vesuvius erupted suddenly, burying the city under more than 15 feet of lava, ash, and mud. A Roman writer named Pliny the Younger witnessed the event from a boat, and wrote about it—the first recorded eruption of Vesuvius. Today Vesuvius is the only active volcano on mainland Europe.

The buried city of Pompeii was discovered in the sixteenth century, but serious excavation did not get underway until 1748, when archaeologists were amazed to find that the whole place had been petrified in mud and ash. The information provided by the astonishingly well-preserved buildings, household objects, jewelry, and artwork present a clear picture of life thousands of years ago. For example, elaborately detailed mosaic hunting scenes show not only beautiful and masterful artistry, but also tell us what kinds of animals were hunted at the time. "Many disasters have befallen the world, but few have brought posterity so much joy," wrote the German poet, Johann Wolfgang von Goethe.

Today visitors can walk along the streets of Pompeii and wander through the ruins of the open forum in the center of the city, through the amphitheatre, marketplace, and villas. Excavation continues today.

L is for the Lava
that flowed one summer day
and froze in time forever
a city called Pompeii.

Maria Montessori (1870–1952) graduated from the University of Rome in 1896. She was the first Italian woman to graduate with a medical degree.

Interested in child development, she began to create new methods of teaching. In 1907 Montessori opened her own school, where her students were preschoolers from poor families. She had so much success with her approach to teaching that eventually she developed her own theory of education. This became known as the Montessori Method.

The Montessori Method is based on the idea that children need different learning environments at different ages and stages, in order to help them best develop independence and intellect. Montessori observed that children up to age six develop through their senses, so they should be encouraged to use touch, sight, hearing, smell, and taste in the classroom. For older students ages six to twelve, the learning environment changes to provide and stimulate abstract ideas, reasoning, and creativity. Students are often encouraged to explore topics independently.

There are still many Montessori schools throughout the world.

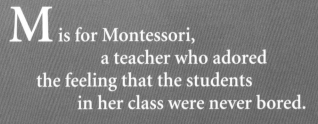

M is for Montessori,
a teacher who adored
the feeling that the students
in her class were never bored.

N n

Naples—or *Napoli*—is the capital of the Campania region. After Rome and Milan, it is the third largest city in Italy. In ancient times, the neighboring Greeks called the city "Neapolis" (new city). The people of Naples are still referred to as Neapolitans.

Raffaele Esposito was a Neapolitan baker. When the king and queen of Italy visited Naples in 1889, Raffaele created a special dish for them. On a piece of flatbread he arranged green basil, white mozzarella cheese, and red tomato sauce, in honor of the Italian flag. Other bakers began to copy this dish right away. Raffaele had invented pizza.

The Museo Archeologico Nazionale is the home of one of the most important archeological collections in the world, bursting with art and artifacts from ancient Greece and Pompeii. Commissioned in 1600 and completed in 1843, Palazzo Reale means "royal palace." Chock-full of beautiful paintings, frescoes, and other treasures, the palace also houses the largest library in southern Italy, the Biblioteca Nazionale.

N is for the city of Naples,
    lively and cosmopolitan.
A native of this city
      is called a Neapolitan.

With its striking turrets and triumphal arch, Castel Nuovo is one of a handful of castles in Naples, the oldest of which is Castel dell'Ovo. "Egg Castle" was begun in 1154, and occupies a small island where a Roman colony once existed. One story has it that the castle came by its name when the poet Virgil placed a magical egg in the foundation to ensure structural stability.

The island of Capri lies at the entrance of the Gulf of Naples in the Tyrrhenian Sea. So legendary is Capri's beauty that the Roman emperors Augustus and Tiberius built villas for themselves there. Greek mythology has it that Capri was home to the Sirens, beautiful sea nymphs whose singing lured unwitting sailors into crashing their boats on the rocks. Capri's Blue Grotto is a famous sea cave. When the sun shines through its water, the grotto illuminates with bright, shimmering, sapphire-blue light.

O is for the Opera
performers sing, not speak.
And singers work for years
to develop fine technique.

Giacomo Puccini

L'elisir d'amore (The Elixir of Love)

Gioachino Rossini

Stradivari Violin

Giuseppe Verdi

Dancer

Antonio Vivaldi

TEATRO ALLA SCALA

IL TURCO IN ITALIA

GIOACHINO ROSSINI

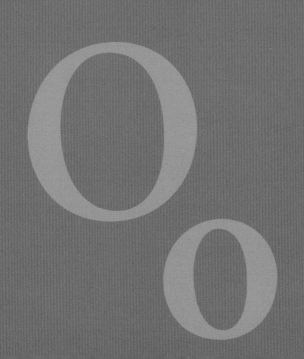
Claudio Monteverdi

Much of the world's greatest music has come from Italy, from the likes of composers Puccini (*Madame Butterfly*), Vivaldi (*The Four Seasons*), Rossini (*The Barber of Seville*), and Verdi (*La Traviata*). Opera, a sumptuous art form in which words in a play are sung instead of spoken, originated in Italy in the 1500s. Groups of musicians and poets in Florence calling themselves *camerata*, inspired by Greek and Roman history, set plays with classical themes to music. By the late 1600s opera had become popular in other parts of Europe.

Italian composers devised a system for writing down music that is still used today. Musicians everywhere use Italian words like *adagio* (slowly), *allegro* (fast and lively), *pianissimo* (soft), and *fortissimo* (loud) to indicate how a piece of music is meant to be played.

The violin was developed in Cremona by the instrument maker Andrea Amati in the 1530s. Antonio Stradivari (1644–1737) was a pupil of Amati's grandson, Nicolò. Stradivari used to take long walks through the forest, looking for the perfect wood to make his violins. He is considered to be a genius craftsman, and his instruments are masterpieces of rare beauty and superior sound. About 400 of his violins exist today.

O
o

In towns and cities across Italy, *piazze* are large open plazas surrounded by buildings. A *piazza* is a place for people to gather at cafes and *trattorias* (restaurants), to shop, to watch street performers, or to sit outside and enjoy a *gelato* (ice cream).

Rome's Piazza Navona is built on top of what was once an ancient stadium used for chariot races and other sporting events. There are still traces of this stadium, built in the first century AD. Of the many *piazze* in Rome, Piazza Navona is the social center of the city. This gorgeous Baroque *piazza* is lined with palaces built hundreds of years ago, and contains a splendid fountain designed by the great sculptor and architect, Gianlorenzo Bernini (1598–1680).

In Verona, Piazza Erbe has been the center of life since ancient times. Named after Verona's old herb market, the marketplace in the *piazza* today still bustles with throngs of vendors and shoppers.

Pp

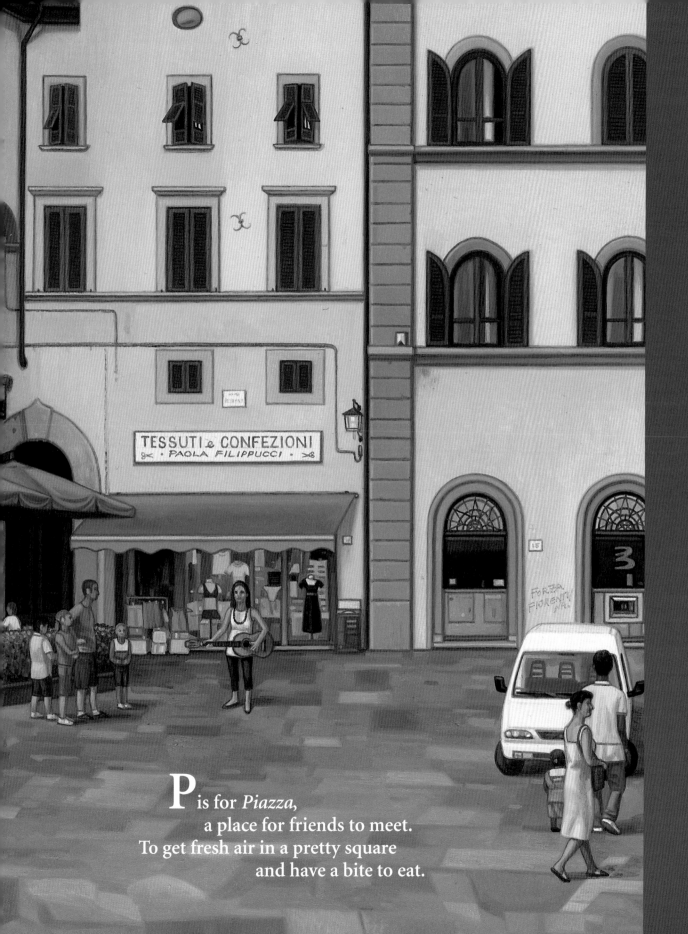

Visitors flock to Piazza San Marco in Venice year-round, especially to see the famous Basilica San Marco and the Palazzo Ducale. The grand *basilica* (church) combines architectural and decorative elements from the East and the West, and it is one of the most interesting buildings in Europe. The gorgeous Palazzo Ducale was once the official home of the *doges* (magistrates or people who administer the law) who ruled Venice in centuries past.

Piazza della Bocca della Verità (*piazza* of the mouth of truth) in Rome is known for the Mouth of Truth, a medieval stone drain cover carved into a face with an open mouth. Legend has it that if you stick your hand into the opening, it will shut tight around the hands of liars.

P is for *Piazza*,
a place for friends to meet.
To get fresh air in a pretty square
and have a bite to eat.

Q is for *Quattrocento*,
when painting and sculpture flourished.
With creativity in the air,
the world was greatly nourished.

Quattrocento (kwa-tro-CHEN-to) is Italian for **400**, and is used to indicate the 1400s—the period of the Renaissance. The Renaissance (1300s–1600) was a movement across western Europe that embraced a new appreciation for the art and literature of ancient Rome and Greece. It produced some of the greatest art in the history of the world—a "rebirth." Italy was the center of the Renaissance.

Renaissance painters were interested in working in a naturalistic style (See F). In order to do this, a technique called "perspective" was needed, to help the artist represent the world in a more realistic way. Perspective is a system for representing three-dimensional space on a flat surface. It is based on the optical illusion that parallel lines appear to meet in the distance.

Architect/writer Leon Battista Alberti (1404–1472) invented a device to aid in this technique. He built a wood frame, then stretched transparent material over it, which he divided into squares with thread. He looked through this "window" at the subject he was going to draw. Onto a piece of paper or canvas with a corresponding grid penciled in, he sketched his subject as it appeared in each little square, thus accurately copying it to scale.

Qq

R is for the city of Rome
whose beauty will astound you.
Modern life is bustling
and antiquities surround you.

Rome is the capital of Italy. This marvelous city has beautiful architecture, sculpture, and fountains from hundreds and thousands of years ago. These antiquities are sprinkled everywhere, alongside fashionable new office buildings, schools, and modern apartment buildings. This juxtaposition of modern and ancient gives Rome a magical feeling of timelessness. It's no wonder that its nickname is "The Eternal City."

The Colosseum was Rome's largest amphitheatre, holding up to fifty thousand people. Dedicated in AD 80 the Colosseum was used for public entertainment and sporting events, much like today's stadiums. On occasion the Colosseum's arena was even filled with water in order to stage battles between ships.

As the center of government, business, and law, the group of buildings known as the Roman Forum was the hub of daily life in ancient Rome. Today you can wander through the ruins of the Roman Forum where life bustled two thousand years ago, and walk where ancient Romans walked—the Curia (Senate House), the Temple of Saturn, the Arch of Septimius Severus, Basilica Julia (*basilica* can also mean church or meeting hall but this one is a courthouse), and many other wondrous sites.

The ancient Romans were seafaring people. Neptune, the god of the sea, was an important figure to them. Neptune is depicted in many fountains throughout Italy, including the Trevi, the most famous fountain in Rome. The Trevi Fountain was designed by Nicola Salvi, based on an earlier design by Bernini who was unable to complete the project when funds ran out. Water to the Trevi Fountain is still supplied by the Aqua Vergine aqueduct, built by Agrippa in 19 BC to supply water to the new Roman baths. Free and open to the public, the popular baths served as fitness clubs and recreation centers, lecture halls, and libraries.

Walking distance from the Trevi is the Piazza di Spagna—Spanish Square—the most famous *piazza* in Rome. It contains the Spanish Steps, a vast set of stairs built in the 1720s and designed by Alessandro Specchi. This remarkably beautiful staircase provides a splendid view of Rome, and is a favorite gathering place for Italians and tourists alike.

In the days before films were filled with the technological wizardry of special effects, good movies were appreciated as seriously as good literature for the important insights they offered through powerful storytelling. Filmmakers were considered as authors. Historic Cinecittà, on the outskirts of Rome, is the largest film studio in Europe. In the years after World War II it was home to a group of important movie directors who started a new movement called "neorealism." The films of Federico Fellini, Vittorio De Sica, Roberto Rossellini, Luchino Visconti, and others told stories about the quiet heroism of ordinary people when faced with life's difficulties.

Michelangelo Buonarroti (1475–1564) was a brilliant leader of the Renaissance. An artistic genius and a true Renaissance—or Universal—man, Michelangelo was a great painter, sculptor, architect, and poet. Like all great Renaissance artists such as Raphael, Titian, and others, Michelangelo valued classical ideals, and studied the art of ancient times.

Michelangelo's sculpture, *David*, depicts the Israelite king. *David* is the largest freestanding marble statue since ancient times.

But Michelangelo's greatest work is the ceiling of the Sistine Chapel in the Vatican (worldwide headquarters for the Catholic Church). He completed hundreds of drawings for the frescoes that would eventually cover the enormous vaulted ceiling of the chapel. The project took four and a half years, partly because Michelangelo dismissed his helpers, whose work he did not think was good enough. He executed the immense job by himself, painting in an uncomfortable position, not allowing anyone in the chapel while he worked.

When the ceiling was completed and unveiled in 1512, people were dumbfounded by its remarkable beauty. Visitors today have the same reaction.

S s

S is for the Sistine Chapel
and its very remarkable ceiling.
Painted by Michelangelo,
with brilliance and great feeling.

T t

When we talk about the economy of a community, a state, or a country, the principle is the same: a way of using resources to produce income. A country must make money to support itself and its citizens just as an individual business or a family must earn money.

Since World War II, as Italy's economy shifted from an agricultural to an industrial one, it has made its way into the top ten world economies. Its most important natural resource is the rich farmland in the Po Valley. Grapes are Italy's most valuable crop, and most of the grapes are used to make wine, which is exported around the world. Italy is also one of the world's leading producers of olives and olive oil. Other crops include wheat, corn, rice, and sugar beets. More than half the world's artichokes come from Italy.

Manufacturing accounts for a large part of the national economy. Most of Italy's manufacturing takes place in the triangle of Milan, Turin, and Genoa, in northwest Italy. Milan—*Milano*—is the capital of the Lombardy region, and Italy's center of finance and international trade. It is the heart of Italy's banking, fashion and design, publishing, and advertising industries. Italy's chief exports include wine and beverages, shoes and clothing, cars, furniture, machinery, and fruits and vegetables.

Soccer

Vespa

Fashion

Cappuccino

Artichoke

Scamorza Cheese

T is for Trade and commerce,
the business side of things.
Like the manufacture of olive oil
and the money that it brings.

U is for Uffizi,
a museum filled with treasure.
The importance of its heritage
is impossible to measure.

The Uffizi (ooh-FEE-tzee) Gallery in Florence houses the world's greatest collection of Italian Renaissance paintings. The collection was assembled over centuries by the Medici family. The Uffizi was originally built as *uffici* (offices) for Duke Cosimo I in the 1500s.

During World War II thousands of pieces of artwork were systematically stolen by Germany's Third Reich. Hundreds of paintings by artists such as Michelangelo, Titian, and Botticelli were stolen from Florence alone. Hundreds of works by da Vinci, Caravaggio, Raphael, and many others were stolen from collections across Italy and Europe. Some were destroyed, some were retrieved, and others are still missing.

In response to this crisis, military officials at the time allowed a special unit of British and American art experts to form the Monuments, Fine Arts and Archives Section—a special force known as the "Monuments Men." Their mission was to protect the great monuments and architecture of Europe, and to return stolen artwork to its rightful place. This important work continues today, as there are thousands of pieces of artwork still missing from the thefts during World War II.

U u

Venice (*Venezia*) is one of the most unusual cities in the world. The capital of the Veneto region, the historic center of Venice sits on more than 100 islands in the Adriatic Sea. The buildings stand not on solid ground, but on wood posts driven into mud. There are no cars or trucks, only pedestrian traffic.

Motorboats and *vaporetti* (water buses) are the main mode of transportation along the more than 150 canals in Venice. Hundreds of bridges connect the islands to one another, and you can get practically anywhere on foot. The Grand Canal is Venice's main canal. Lined with palaces built over a period of five centuries, the Grand Canal winds majestically through the heart of the city.

Gondolas—long, slim, flat boats pushed along with poles—have been part of Venetian life since the eleventh century, but now they are expensive and used mostly by tourists.

V is for the city of Venice,
no cars or trucks in sight.
Imagine how the Grand Canal
catches the morning light.

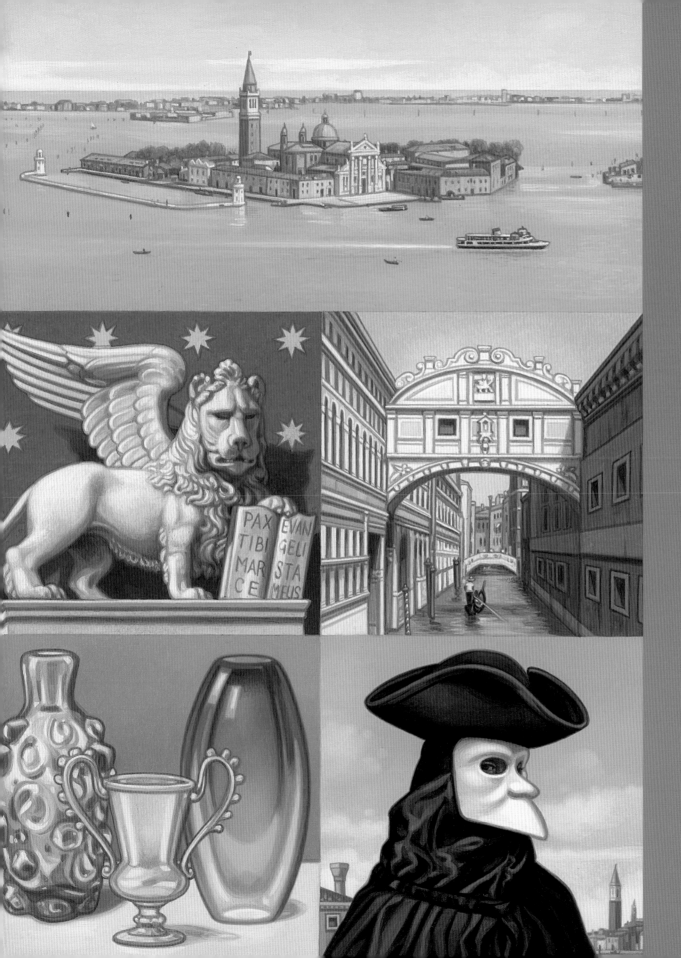

Part of Venice is located on the mainland. The majority of Venetians live in the mainland communities of Mestre and Marghera. Here there are more job opportunities, the cost of living is lower, and many people prefer the modern apartment buildings to the older architecture of the islands, where there is no room for new construction.

Sadly, Venice is threatened by the slow destruction caused by flooding and pollution. During the winter months, storms cause flood damage to the buildings and public squares. Also, constant exposure to water weakens the foundations of Venice's buildings. People across the world have joined various organizations to help solve this problem.

Around the time of the navigator Christopher Columbus's (1451–1506) explorations, Europeans knew very little about the world outside of Europe. Their ideas were based on a map of the world made in ancient times by the astronomer Ptolemy, which mistakenly showed that most of the world was covered by land, not water. When Columbus set off from Spain in 1492 on the first of four voyages across the Atlantic Ocean, his expedition included three wooden ships and ninety crew members. Based on his concept of geography, Columbus mistook the Americas for the East Indies.

Venetian Marco Polo (1254–1324) traveled to China (then called Cathay) with his businessmen father and uncle. Fluent in four languages, Marco conducted official business for Mongol ruler Kublai Khan, and eventually wrote a book about China.

Florentine explorer Amerigo Vespucci (1454–1512) mistakenly claimed that his travels had taken him to a "New World" where he explored the American mainland. A German mapmaker named Martin Waldseemuller, believing this account, put Vespucci's name on a map in 1507, which is how America got its name.

W is for Wanderlust,
the love of exploration.
Curiosity about the world
and a nose for navigation.

X is for the number ten
and M is for a thousand.
Latin was the language then,
before there was Italian.

Besides being the 24th letter of our alphabet, X is the Roman numeral for 10. In the Roman numeral system all numbers are written with a combination of seven symbols: I (1), V (5), X (10), L (50), C (100), D (500), and M (1,000). There is no symbol for zero.

The number system we use for counting and calculating is the decimal system. The word "decimal" comes from a Latin word meaning "of tenths." It is thought that this number system comes from the earliest method of counting—on fingers. "Digit," another word for number, comes from the Latin word for finger, *digitus*.

The decimal system is based on powers of 10, with each number place increasing by a power of ten. The number 1,987 means one thousand, nine hundreds, eight tens, and seven ones.

These days we use Roman numerals to carve dates on monuments and buildings. They are also still used on clocks and in outlines.

IL CALENDARIO

Y is for a Year and its months.
How did they come to be?
Knowing a bit about Latin
and mythology is the key.

January - *Gennaio*

February - *Febbraio*

March - *Marzo*

April - *Aprile*

May - *Maggio*

June - *Giugno*

July - *Luglio*

August - *Agosto*

September - *Settembre*

October - *Ottobre*

November - *Novembre*

December - *Dicembre*

SALSA DI POMODORO

Did you know that all the names of our months have Roman origins?

January is named after Janus, the Roman god of beginnings. He was responsible for daybreak, and generally for all human endeavors or undertakings. **February** is named after *Februa*, the festival or month of purification. **March** is named for Mars, the god of war. Romans called **April** *Aprilis*. This name could have come from the word meaning "to open" or possibly from Aphrodite, the goddess of love. **May** probably got its name from the goddess of spring, Maia. **June** is thought to have gotten its name from Juno, the goddess of marriage.

July is named for Roman general Julius Caesar. The Romans called this month Julius. **August** was named for Emperor Augustus. **September** was originally the seventh month on the Roman calendar, and its name comes from the Latin word for seven, *septem*. Likewise, **October**, **November**, and **December** get their names from the Latin words for numbers. *Octo* is eight, *novem* is nine, and *decem* is ten. December became the twelfth month of the year on a later Roman calendar.

Yy

Z is for Zabaglione,
a delightful Italian treat.
Made with sugar and eggs,
cooked 'til it's ready to eat.

Recipe for Zabaglione (Zah-bah-**lyo**-nay)

4 egg yolks
4 teaspoons sugar
4 tablespoons Marsala wine

Whisk all ingredients over a double-boiler until thickened like pudding. Take on and off the heat while cooking so as not to scramble the eggs. Serve warm. Buon Appetito!

—Compliments of Chef Mario Batali

The food of Italy is praised for its use of fresh, seasonal, and local ingredients. This approach to cooking makes Italian cuisine one of the most popular in the world.

Dessert is perhaps the least important part of an Italian meal. It is common practice in many restaurants to offer nothing fancier than a savory piece of locally made cheese and some fresh fruit at the end of a meal. Traditionally, sweet desserts are associated with special occasions such as holidays and family celebrations.

Italy does produce a constellation of marvelous desserts. For the most part, they are fairly simple and not overly fussy. Traditional cakes and puddings are plain but delicious. *Zuccotto* is a dome-shaped pound cake covered with chocolate whipped cream. This recipe comes from Florence and reminds people of the famous Brunelleschi dome. *Tiramisù* ("pick-me-up") is an espresso-soaked cakey-pudding. *Torta Sbrisolona* ("crumbly cake") is a beautifully traditional cake made with cornmeal, simple and not too sweet. *Gelato* (ice cream) is very popular. *Panna Cotta* ("cooked cream") —a soft, smooth pudding—is another scrumptiously simple dish. Desserts using fresh, seasonal fruits are also extremely popular, like orange slices soaked in lemon juice and sugar, and apple fritters.

To Edda Gusman

ELISSA

To the memory of my magnificent Italian-immigrant parents and parents-in-law

MARIO

To my ABC: Anna, Bibi, and Giovanni

MARCO

ACKNOWLEDGMENT

The illustrator would like to thank the people who posed and helped in gathering references for this project: Paolo Caneva, Ilaria Celigo, Laura Filippucci, Marisa Murgo, Anna Giulia Ventura, Francesca Ventura, Giovanni Ventura, Paolo Ventura, and Piero Ventura.

Sleeping Bear Press
310 North Main Street, Suite 300
Chelsea, MI 48118
www.sleepingbearpress.com

© 2009 Sleeping Bear Press is an imprint of Gale, a part of Cengage Learning.

Printed and bound in the United States.

10 9 8 7 6 5 4 3 2

Library of Congress Cataloging-in-Publication Data

Cuomo, Mario Matthew.
C is for ciao : an Italy alphabet / written by Governor Mario Cuomo and Elissa D. Grodin ; illustrated by Marco Ventura.
p. cm.
Summary: "Each letter of the alphabet represents a topic related to Italy. Topics include: aqueducts, Da Vinci, Florence, Montessori, the Sistine Chapel, and zabaglione. A poem introduces each letter topic and expository side-bar text provides details"—Provided by publisher.
ISBN 978-1-58536-361-2
1. Italy--Juvenile literature. 2. Alphabet books. I. Grodin, Elissa, 1954- II. Ventura, Marco. III. Title.
DG417.C86 2009

945—dc22   2008031974